There once was a young yak
who hated trying new foods.

One day, the young yak's father gave her a yellow banana.

"YUCK!" yelled the yak without
even taking a bite.
The yak tossed the yellow banana
into her neighbor's yard.

The young yak's father
gave her some yogurt.

"YUCK!" yelled the yak.
She tossed the yogurt into her neighbor's yard.

The young yak's father gave her a yam.

"YUCK!" yelled the yak.
She tossed the yam into her neighbor's yard.

A wise old yak lived next door to the young yak.
He was in his yard playing with his yo-yo.

The yam hit the wise old yak right in the head!
"YIKES!" yelled the wise old yak.

"YOO-HOO, young yak!"
the wise old yak yelled over the fence.
"Yes?" said the young yak.
"You should taste things before you yell yuck,"
said the wise old yak.

The young yak leaped over the fence into her neighbor's yard.

She tasted the yellow banana,
the yogurt, and the yam.
"YOWEEE!" said the young yak.
"These are yummy!"

And now she's the yak who yells,
"YUM!"

Yy Cheer

Y is for yo-yo, Y is for yak
Y is for a yummy yogurt snack
Y is for yarn, yes, yard, and young
Y is for yam and a bright yellow sun
Hooray for big Y, small y, too—
the letter that makes you want to yell
     "YAHOO!"